NAKED WANTING

Naked

CAMINO DEL SOL *A Latina and Latino Literary Series*

MARGO TAMEZ

Wanting

THE UNIVERSITY OF ARIZONA PRESS *Tucson*

The University of Arizona Press
© 2003 Margo Tamez
First Printing
All rights reserved
⊚ This book is printed on acid-free,
archival-quality paper.
Manufactured in the United States of America
Design and composition by Jeff Clark
at Wilsted & Taylor Publishing Services

08 07 06 05 04 03   6 5 4 3 2 1

Library of Congress Cataloging-in-Publication Data
Tamez, Margo.
    Naked wanting / Margo Tamez.
        p. cm. — (Camino del sol)
    ISBN 0-8165-2248-0
    I. Title. II. Series.
    PS3570.A446 N35 2003
    811'.6—dc21
                        2002013481

British Library Cataloguing-in-Publication Data
A catalogue record for this book is available
from the British Library.

FOR JUS, NAGO, MIM-A-POO, AND BUBBA-CHUH

The great dark is closing in.

Now neither the seer's pride nor the scribe's claptrap.

I'm pouring bowls of light over my head,

I can look at the sun and not be blinded.

And perhaps — what a pity —

> *the most beautiful lie*

> *Will no longer seduce me.*

NAZIM HIKMET

CONTENTS

The following poems appeared or will appear in these maga-
zines or anthologies: *Americas Review,* "Beetles in Bright
Light"; *Sister Nations* (Minnesota Historical Society Press),
"One At A Time," and "Limp Strings"; *Feathers, Fins & Fur*
(Outrider Press), "Between These Worlds" (in another
form); *Stories from Where We Live: The Gulf Coast* (Milkweed
Editions), "My Mother Returns To Calaboz"; *The Missouri
Review,* "Romantic," "Valentine's Day," "The Sound of Doves,"
and "On the Wing."

   I would like to thank the Arizona Commission on the Arts
and the Alice Longon Foundation for their generous support.
My gratitude to Erika Lenz and Jan Selving, whose patient
efforts helped shape these poems and this collection. Special
thanks go to Marta Boswell and Speer Morgan at *The Missouri
Review,* and to Arthur Vogelsang at *American Poetry Review*
for their mindful reading of selected poems. Most humble
regards to Norman Dubie, Beckian Fritz-Goldberg, Alberto
Alvaro Rios, and Jeannine Savard for foundations and gifts.
And, eternally, to my supportive family.

QUIETLY

THROUGH

US

A Species

I

At the jagged-knife edge of a maguey
I glisten on blue, thick skin, like orgasm
in the nectar-swollen labia, monsoon
heat inside the throb, wet
pulp that is before, and after
all that was needed to become.

The prongs open widely,
lift like muscular thighs
to receive the sun's movement.

2

I lived in a womb
that grieved a fetus.
My mother never spoke
of the dead.

Instead she picked at her cuticles,
made the frayed edges peel back,
exposing a flesh,
pink and firm, like salmon.

In church, my father
grabbed one of her hands.
Cupped it firmly between his.
To stop her.

I looked at her hands
when we sat in the pew,

the only memory of her
sitting down. She resisted.

At mass, her shrouded eyes
accused not heavenward, but eye-level
through the webbed sockets
of her black veil.

She was the abyss.
There were animals inside her,
ancient and dark
as the ocean floor.

I was conceived in the womb
of a woman disturbed
with a man
she called life.
Born from a body
that swallows a child,
like a throat that aches
when it pushes back grief.

3

I peer over the tired Formica table,
its wide chrome rim rutting my breasts.
Chin against the smooth cold,
I watch her hands—
the snap of palm,
flesh of her wrist,
a tortilla from hand to hand.
I inhale the balmy butter.

I think a secret:
this is how you give.

I eat,
and the body is mine.

4

The hands return and return,
mend holes in small dresses,
look for patent-leather shoes
I lost at St. Thomas More,
find the cigar box I hid under my bed,

my hair clips, and pieces of her
Mexican jewelry inside.
Her hands stab large, black pins
through the thick coil of her bun,
hold a small cloth-bound book of the Virgin
she bought at a yard sale,
palm-size sewn covers,
the frescos my fingertips memorize.
All these I put away in my box
and fasten the lid on the scent
of stale cigars.

5

She grinds herbs down to powder.
Her granite *molcajete,**

---

*Aztecan mortar and pestle

is the beginning of us. She
remakes her family in this bowl.

The ground-up garlic, cumin, and coriander
scent her house,
rise into my brain,

place her in my dream.
In the dream she is sleeveless, she smiles
and cuts her long black hair
for my sister's birthday,
each strand of hair
tied to a balloon . . .

6

I came from moon-eyes.
Pushed through the membrane,
slipped out songs of wailing woman.

I dream:

water
from the abyss
flows her
through me.

First Choice

You ask me which shovel I want to use,
give me first choice.
I pick the one with a worn handle;
its length suits my height.
I know I won't get splinters —
the wood, seasoned with years
of your skin and sweat.

Our first garden, a second marriage.
We feel what we want, shy to say it all.
This is like making love,
the first time conceiving.

At the gin, we fill a truck's bed high with mulch,
some laughter, mostly wordless labor,
the slicing sound of the blades in earth,
our jeans dusty up to the knees.
The repeated arcs of quiet arms,
your eyelids.

We unload it all into our field.

Milagro

My son shows a thin line, light and scent,
on the crease of his neck.
Palo verde — faint salt and weedy —
pulses between my nose and upper lip.

During his bath, he loops
water swirls with his slick black hair.
He swings his head around and up,
thrusting with the conviction
of a Heavy Metal fan.

My vocation by the tub
is to watch out for him.
He sees buoyancy unfurl,
the plastic donuts spring back
and splash his face.
His cub hands push
under water.

I want him to finish,
a quickie, so I might
get to things in my head.
His lassos of water
O's and thick worms flying through air,
colliding into the shower curtain,
reorganize and bead into droplets
shivering towards one another
and spool into threads as if being unwound
by gravity's thick hand
forcing them to swim and enter her,

disappearing in the tub of water.
My toes curl,
dig divots
inside leather slip-ons.

Can't I be still,
towel in hand
to wrap his soft curves,
and hold him
to hear his heart?

When I think of it I do,
and how many times I don't,
thinking of everything else.
This is how he and I might uncoil,
everything else,
rushing him,
digging in.

Milpa

The bald spot at the back
of my daughter's head
is neither blank nor bare.
Delicious, the velvet of it,
as my tongue on the season's
first ripe peach.
The tiny hairs'
faint scent, like Brie.
Here are her birthmarks,
rosy constellations beneath the pale down,
ovals of cosmic gusts
only four months in our universe.
Planets mapped themselves
on her skull's thin cloak.

At night in bed
she rubs her head
this way and that,
eyes fastening her memory
to my world.

More stars appear every night
as the soft hairs, in time,
wear away.
I like to watch her firm nods,
right and left. So certain.
As if to drive away
the nots,
the no you can'ts.

Quilt Woman

I am there in the wood patch,
its pattern like Navajo sand prayers.
Another thrift-store prize,
my daughter inflates the quilt
with determined sighs.
Her body, like a small walrus on shore,
rolls and pushes through the grids and folds
all her volumes:
thighs, rolls of stomach,
bud breasts, tube toes.
She pipes sound like breeze
under the blanket I hold
open like a tent. Coming all the way,
her face rises,
glances at me with a hmmm,
and she rolls over again,
wiggles back through,
appraising me. I think:
she'll keep me.

An Inevitable Parallel

A red-tailed hawk returns.
She affirms another season is coming.

A twin engine sprays above us.
Tonight the humidity will thicken
the chemical cocktail
seeping into the air ducts.

Down the road my stepson shrieks
while my husband combs lice from his hair,
an infestation.

A thousand miles farther,
my oldest son dreams that ants fall from Mars.
He walks barefoot along a canal.
His hands reach into silt water
for time.

He can't catch it. Dreams being that way.

A hawk returns from the long summer in the north.
Her flyway runs parallel with the cotton,
the cotton parallel to itself,
the farm tenants,
and future tenants
in a master-planned community . . .

The hawk on the barbed wire lifts,
her talons grasp and thrust several times,

slashing crisp air.
Her neck and back thicken when she hastens,
feathers, eyelids, beak, jaw, wings — all fractals
of fundamental wanting,
her prey expectant and within grasp.

Beetles in Bright Light

I

My son came in a stumble,
teetering on thick feet
along the curve of an even path.
Ran to the calves of my legs.
His head pushed between the buckle
of my knees and thighs, my dress,
sucked upward, whipped my face
and stung.

He ran, not knowing the small plane
would not land on him. The body
so near our heads, propelling
upward, back arched,
carved quarter-moons in an aching sky.
Spewed light and liquid. We watched
that thin line expand with air,
swathe the field, then blend.
Silent as it dissolved into earth. As it
left our sight, it became us.

2

A Swainson's hawk sees the field with her mind —
what is necessary. She will eat.
Her blade eyes snap toward a pocket gopher
as he reaches up through brittle stubble
for soft fibers, their cells still moist.
Gnaws into the core of crisp stalks,

chews fallen seeds,
chances on something to eat, what remains
on the cotton raked from its pod, and
the startled branches —
what the machines couldn't reach.

3

I sat in this thrift chair before with another child,
and it was dusk, the chair freshly painted,
though it was rusty underneath. I was hurried,
wanting the new colors. One day it broke
from decay, and joined other useless relics
in the bone pile.
With the other child, the sky
was a fleshy womb of purple and red veins,
the sun tumbling backwards
behind the sawed edge of mountains.
The child forming inside me was soft,
exquisite, unexpectant.

4

Time skips and disturbs the beetles
pricking their way across the ground.
They do not stop. They are relentless
to complete something begun.

I have heard about Reason.
Though it sounds like a medieval device,
a dodge, a ploy, subterfuge,
being stuck on worn-out ideas. The ideas

below human potential. So cheap, they get used anyway.
The practitioners ignore how the damage multiplies.
Will not admit the killing.

The beetles.
I watch them, lift my feet,
stay out of the way, and wonder
about my womb. It is marked.
The cancer sets its bleak scene.

5

He runs,
looks for my arms, legs,
tries to climb, holds me
with his unsteady balance,
clutches my dress. I move us
to the furrows of carrots and beets.
He pulls at their tops, forgets
more as he walks along. The buzz
moves to the next field,
its chemical advances from the body,
then quietly through us.

FOR

KEEPS

The Wait

Twenty-eight days and a face.
A new face again, perhaps.
I feel signs of this new who.
A who? What?
(his expressive face)
Perhaps, more birth.

I will love, love, if you are alive . . .
We move like shadows of ourselves
inside other selves —
I embrace you tentatively.

Nursing's got me wrung out.
These stretch marks don't extend
my will to be a house
so soon, again.

I am like the chain of hives
across my stomach —
irritated and raw.

To possibility
and more change (he says,
this is his love).

Face of moon or face of child?

Inhaling Two Worlds

The black wheel of the steering column
vibrates from the engine up my spine,
shaking threads that barely connect
one place to another—
desires to actions, promises to delivery,
me to the child I carry.

Black rubber, the tires melt the morning.
I'm gummed to this machine—
wires, axles, hot oil in its gut.
I move into traffic, but want
to hear music of mallows. Courageous
and wild. I want forgiving strokes
I've felt lying on sweet grass, its mesh
with my hair. I'd rather be picking young peas
off the trellis, eating them
sweet with life.

The gases from the street infect me;
all I am is unthreading.
Where I enter the pavement
every traffic light stalls.

One at a Time

Autumn 1997, for Angelito

There is a hunger for order
but a thirst against.

    LINDA GREGG, "A Thirst Against"

I

Two crisp sunflowers are small enough
and fit into the weave
of your palm-size casket.

I am pouring you into water.
The equinox, midwifery,
and practical herbs
unravel the flesh between us.
I felt you
and still
you enclose me.
I bargain with God for a reversal.
Life's fragility, the inflexible end
excessive.

The small altar on the counter.
Votives hover around me,
my body an apparition, hermetic,
like you, just that far
off from my grasp. You
go through me everywhere.
You will pass to spirit in four days.

2

I herd goats from the crisp cornfield.
June's last planting, they munch the fodder,
eyeing me, unwilling to be stopped,
though I was competent.
They saw my stick
and turned tail,
straight to their corral.
They're pissed, but put up with it.

The strain in my pelvis became hard
after the hog's regular feeding.
Getting him fattened
for a spring slaughter.

I walk a different path back,

notice a familiar scent—astringent stamen,
red vulvas in the season's devil claws
release their love-juice
for the pollinators. A cluster
eaten bare
by a moth's tenacious mouth.

Entering, and re-entering.
All the world shifts.
I bend to draw in their scent,
press my face into their pollen.
Their scent is on me,
and I back up,
nearly falling to the ground,
the scent evocative,
I pluck a handful and rush away.

Think: *déjà vu, something or*
someone full of seed
is coming toward me.

The bugles of a tobacco tree
trumpet a faded yellow song.
I follow a worn path to the house,
gather new corn pollen,
elder going to berry.

3

All the candles in the house self-extinguish.
The ones from Mexico, hand-painted "Tú y Yo,"
the last ones to go,
tiny wicks curling under the clear pool of wax.
My husband asks, *are you ready?*
We walk onto the moist ground
he prepares for ceremony.

You are sacred,
this life we gave you
taken.

I pull on a chair to stand,
tremor like an unraveling rope
that gets away
no matter where my hands grasp.
Me, you, his eyes, his look.
I know again

how awful this becomes.
He looks up at sky,
a weightless altar,

the sun witnesses what happens,
and I don't feel better,
prayers, rituals
don't stop this shriveling,
this anger, this fist I become.

For Keeps

for Milagro

In the opening petal of your eye, my face is a head,
a large face, larger than the rest of me.

I tremble at the reflection I cast—
distorted in your cornea, my head is colossal,

my chest a tapering stem. I reject my
diminished chest. I want to

be naked, unafraid,
to show you my defeats, the wanting

when my body was an oily slick
in thin water, no merging

between me and language,
me and the never heard, never known,

restless pulses that cut me away
and would not vaporize if wished for.

How loud the silences really are,
piling on each other,

with faces showing regrets,
the undone, or the pushed away and

once-believed-in attachments.
Like thin-throated specters, they quiver

their accusations, mount each other,
dig in hard, and rock in the genital ooze.

All the things I let die, or killed,
getting screwed.

I never knew
this hunger against silence

would resurrect my dead,
lay down the genealogy between fear, denial,

clumsiness, disregard,
the sweet breath between our lips,

ropy flesh between mother and child,
one's grief, the other's mutiny,

we gamble away each other's promise,
and promises, then fear when we have to pay

for the damage we commit,
keep telling our children

we can change
we can change

ourselves, this world
and make it a promise to keep.

In the Floodplain

We walk with hands clasped lightly.
We don't know each other well yet.
I feel the moisture on yours
blend with mine.

I've wanted to show you this place
for some time. I would walk out here
to find something, not knowing
where to go, then come to see
there is much more I find
when not looking.

Stones the shapes of gourds,
reminding me to water
the field you planted.
The curve of ironwood on the faces
of leaves. A jackrabbit on his side,
resting, that is really an old mesquite stump
washed bare by time.

Because fractal theory is on my mind,
and there it is, the map of the basin
on every surface of the desert floor.

They were all caught in a flood, a force
that marks them, the imprint
a pattern of remembrance,
a need to mark passage. Decay

and continuance reins life
in the floodplain.

We are swirled
in we are swirled in
we swirl.

Witness of Birds

The shy witness of birds
Darting behind the leaves.

JEANNINE SAVARD, *Snow Water Cove*

1

First a wing's push against my satchel;
in disbelief
I hear and feel it all:
a press of tiny, clawed feet
climbing my back,
then the bowl curve of dawn.

The dwarf cowbird announces a pessimistic note,
thrusts me against a swirl,
and we are both clutching sky.
Snared into spines of a short yucca,
I see her land in a nearby mesquite, launch again,
with an undeniable purpose — to mess with me.
I'm being singled out, all debts called in.
I'm caught alone in the open.

The day workers across the street
witness this tangle. Feeling stupid, I think:
this is weird. This bird is breaking
the division between spirits and mortals.
Stranger still, they get it. Laugh at me.

2

The parking lot is empty. Across the road,
undocumented Mexicans wait, hopeful, on a corner.
They are exposed dangerously, risk

family, hunger, assault
out in the open,
hawking their backs, hands, experience.
Their laughter, like small buckets, gurgles,
pájaro! pájaro!*
They point surprise and belief
toward me,
the one inside the pretty dress.

Close to an orange tree,
the clawed push again, the snagging grasp on my hair,
a caw snatching small gulps of wind.
I'm in a sweat of confusion
and fear; my arms thrash at the sky
to break contact,

then fall to my sides suddenly
weighted, numb. I tell myself
to stop resisting the bird,
just run.

*bird! bird!

In the Green Trailer

My eyes watch the road
through a frayed curtain.
Think: *I am a bandit.*
The occasional semi
makes the world
outside the rez
far away.

Through the lace's stitched eyes
shadows rise like weightless skins,
move the air where everything falls
on the surface
as if detained,
like stories
I don't tell him. This
and dust of the Huhukam
blow through sills of cardboard panels
and cheap aluminum siding.

The trailer's not tied
to this patch of creosote and sand
that defies my stare.

Without electricity, another monsoon,
I check the road often, survey the damage.
I could walk to another trailer down the dirt road,
the nearest phone. The truck will never make it,
the mud too deep and loose.

He drove to the border
to bring workers.
The days from then,

this month, the next,
blur like heat and diesel
fanning above the road.

I am shadow behind a crease,
talking to the invisible him.

I might walk to the window
nine times today.
Nine times nine days
is eighty-one movements
towards making it
through another heat wave.

The heat is wild,
I try to distract myself,
quoting loudly to a kangaroo rat
who ate the last dried chiles,
the scientists know
the boreal forest carbon sinks are melting,
carbon-release ratios are at their worst
in nine thousand years. I feel gutsy,
hatching deals with translucent spiders,
their bellies and the pane rattling.
They have the power
to toss this trailer
if I show an attitude.

Another day, I watch
the lizards' swift race
from the scarce shade
of one creosote to the next.
Their faces' acute quivers,
their eyes' abrupt dilation,

dart when they decide
to run their hearts out
to more shade-giving brush.

The time for waterbirds
to come, to lay their eggs,
is the same time moving
the shade tree, the lizard,
the scorched land,
and the ocean it sucks
into its withering stomach.

The same time moves the curtain's flutter and dangles
on the snake-line in my face,
a smooth brown stone.
I become gathered
as my fingers through my hair.
I become the bobbin
of these veined and rough hands.

Limp Strings

I am driving home, the weekend ahead,
planting garlic and grading essays
on the brain. Did he get to the dishes, or
are they piled to greet me? Milpa cries,
her mouth's wet rim quivers, echoes
my jangled pessimism — a wicked necklace,
the O of her mouth comes to me fast
before a six-hundred-acre blur
of alfalfa and sky.
I try not to swerve, my fingers
snatch her overall buckles,
her face bobs like a doll loose at its hinges.
Steering with my knee, stick popped in neutral,
her shoulder and arm I pull to bring her over,
a fast look to the road, lift and remove her
from the second-hand car seat.

Think: *most accidents happen within a mile or two of home.*
I read in a doctor's office.
Hoist her one more time across my lap,
under the wheel, my buttons unfastened.
Rose-lips root around my breast and draw down the milk,
her free hand considers the other nipple.

Flutter in her feet,
her fingers pinch hard,
stretch the dark nipple,
until it goes numb, then crisp . . .

I see myself like a *Mad Magazine* cartoon,
a distorted body,

where you know it's the mind
that is the real subject.
When telling stories, I refer to my boobs
as two long and limp strings
to cheer myself.
If I didn't wear a shirt to conceal them,
they would flap like shoestrings
in the monsoon winds of August.
My husband hears and watches me say this.
Rolls his eyes.
He likes flapjacks.

The Light Is What Is

Quiet is such effort
and glows like hydrogen,
then fades into a crumble,
a fissured clay wall.
From there chants in rose,
coming like patience
for the parched fibers of remembrance:
bougainvillea, dove feathers, and human hair,
the colors of foxtail and amaranth.
These find each other and hold,
spun by an early monsoon,
whipped clockwise up a tunnel of air,
then left near a ceiling of ray to fall,
without falling — more a slow, swaying drift,
a delicate chime
that is its own joy.
Their fibrous alliance welcomes decay.
Woven in a moment with sun.
I see only a language of color and fiber
intensifying spectrum.
What I see ahead,
better than before.
Those that went.
A time to die.

BRINGING

BACK

THE

BIRDS

Bringing Back the Birds

It is time to go Outside, farther than we have ever gone before.
It is time to hear the seabirds singing at the edge of the world
and to bring them back, freshly . . . into our dreams.

GARY P. NABHAN, *Cultures of Habit*

I

The narrow silt road
emerges from a trail
west of a trash mound,
though hardly anyone knows.
Just some elders
from this side of the river.

I saw a crane
behind a mesquite,
and she turned the colors of river rocks.

The sun's evening light
on the rocks' upturned bellies
makes them turtles, pomegranates, and beetles.

I follow the trail beyond old LPs
in the trash heap,
their jagged edges marking the sky.

Ribboned oil slicks,
old medicine bottles,
torn mattresses that expose
what the animals leave inside.

2

Waterbird-women come to lay eggs
before the time for night blankets,
when amaranth seeds fall.

Ravens caw ahead
to other ravens,
and a hundred red-winged blackbirds
braid a communal body.

Sudden hum
wings touching
wings in swift turn
hush
a fast red out of the flux.

3

Among the stones, by tall cattail,
are the ancient faces of toads.
I have a large toad stone that is a sentinel
over the grave of my child.
His surface is pitted
by centuries,
though he holds on.

I channel water to the lilies
and reset him when the rain
shifts his position.

At the river,
the old river before the white man's dam
and then no water,

when I was a girl,
I listened to Waterbird-woman.

All day I placed my fingers
on the stones
and undersides of leaves,
where she left me . . .
where sky pulls herself apart
to show the blisters,
presses her vulva
against creosote,
their broken limbs
green, flesh open,

the stunned air.
Creosotes' netted heads shudder slightly
against little pouts of wind.

4

Roadrunner—
shade & light
shade & light
—catches lizard,

whose warm belly
breathes through it,

breathes . . .
fast first, his skin swirls like scrotum,
soft green purse, then shell color,
soft still cushion.

5

Cicadas in ironwoods,
their constant noise
of need.

6

In the cattail,
where sometimes Waterbird-woman
lays eggs,
mesquite stems have fallen.
I turn them over,
feel the undersides with my fingertips,
the fragile swerves. Swerves of stones.
Swerving water.

In the sun inside my eyes,
heat and glow,
I watch the tiny amoebic floaters.
Inside closed eyelids.

On my small apron,
an embroidered Inca dove

woos: In the dream,
we are at the edge of a shore,
a place a long time ago.

The sky.

The ocean . . .

This is the place where we live.

7

I see a possible earth.
One that we love.
Where we are liable
for the damages
freighted on her.

We are in the tenuous grasp
of lush carnal dreams,
almost awakening.

And here we try to re-enter the dream,
the frothy orgasm reachable,
thrashing against wakefulness.

8

By the canal

I wake early, walk over furrows with bare feet;
a worn-through shift that early dew clings to
sucks my body's heavy extended egg.

I see a crane
standing in the canal.
She is taller than a man.

My adopted Pima uncle clears another field,
his tractor pulling the furrows
to a stretched V.
He recedes, and stays in place.

The sun's gold-blood fingers
rake colors from the rows.

The rows stun me
with their fast, bright panic.

Waterbird, her slanted eyes,
head cocked half away,
half toward me,
weaves her ruby-black wings
in the shining-above world,
where the hanging spools
rattle against each other
like femurs,
all in an arc.

Hanging tentatively like wind chimes,
sound, no sound.
Sound, no sound. And on and on
like that.

The Lightness

I see a web in the epazote
that my husband almost tills down, and
I remember to collect its seed.

A small, complete web,
dusk-light gossamer,
like a hundred needle-thin tubes
of blown glass. I calm my breathing
as my fingers rub the thin stems,
careful not to detach the web.

My palm catches the seeds, tiny orbs
that fall and sieve
through octagons of light.
Crisp pin-leaves,
tentative on spun ladders, spiral past
the one dry body,
its soul without imprint.

Only its frame and a broken wing
are enmeshed and hang
by near-invisible strands.

Cricket's Eye

A flittering veil-wing,
her tube body

moist. Shining along the narrow ridge of its neck,

cricket looks at the girl in church
who is biting
thin silver links of the rosary.

The girl presses her creamy ceramic beads
on the soft skin
between her nose and upper lip,

and chants with the mass:
Blessed art thou among women.

She rolls them one at a time
along her skin
that covers the neck bone and throat.

Traces, with the bare touch
of her fingertip,
hair-thin lines of sweat and earth
that coil in her neck's creases,

winding a swirl,
winding in.

Blessed art thou among women
Blessed is the fruit
Of thy womb . . .

The girl raises her hand to the window ledge
to catch cricket.
Her fingers tremble slightly.
But cricket jumps farther away
into the dark.

A Speed Zone, Inside Out

Utah, 1992

Sometimes the ravens are blurred objects
dwelling in a place that says this can be retrieved.

The road ahead is a false lure of wet asphalt,
while the odometer clicks
to a sliding moment,
infinite as air in front of the fender.

I have to stop.

The gravel beneath me is small rocks rutting small rocks.
A raven, wounded, moves weakly —
striving.

I watch.
I am just the taught things, and put to work
sizing up his claws and beak. Great-grandma
liked slippery black-blue feathers,
practical tokens down the road.
She would feel more of its body,
the warm blood pulsing.

This is a burn-out.
The trek from Salt Lake to Phoenix
a greedy haul.
Pollen and dust a skirt

around my knees. I hover over raven and watch
to the last breath of his life.

Raven caws of warning, she'd say.
Quetzal* leaves the roadkill,
and I offer a tobacco, saying a prayer,
take possession, clench.

One boot heel anchored on the chest cavity,
I tear wings from the back,
the heart from the center.

The exquisite part.

One she believed to be
a sanctuary.

*bird-spirit

Romantic

A bull snake's six-foot coil muscles the soil
in curls and messes. His tail is narrow,
pointed, and taut.
I'm relieved he's not a rattler.

I stand still over him,
ok, no problem, you be here,
I'll move down the path,
his length woven around
limbs of September's last Roprecos,
the remaining tomatoes dark, moist,
cool, near the earth where a sweet scent
implies everything is rotting: *romantic.*
The phosphorescent trunks swelling like throats
that spew green beads of nightshade dew.

The lizard beneath the vitex's blooms
of violet skirts has a throat
in between birth and contraction.
Swirling like scrotum,
stirring S's, the arched waves
above and below rippled flesh.
The lizard's hazel eyes are horizontal slants
like a secret in my head,
the lizard I see in my husband's face.

Is this the last monsoon
or is this autumn? I don't know

when a season, a moment,
a breath
is anything different
than what it is. Change
is just change.

The Earth Walk

Far into the dream, you are the universe.
Black moth, orb.
Like a dark ochre pod, resilient.
Your weaving, a simple cloak
of leaving and returning.

If I could do the same
at the end of my earth walk,
be sheltered in a chrysalis
to dissuade predators,
I'd ask a covenant from my family
to let me go in peace to dream.

To the separation,
larvae, to moth.

Cicada's Walk

I

Short snatched moments. The melons
left unwatered, stunted, lacking leafy growth
to shade them from burn in zone nine.

She in the field all day,
still swollen after birthing her eggs.
Her skin molted, death imminent,
she ate one unripe melon.
Ate it with her thirsty tongue, before the burn.
She thinks: *good, it's wet, so good*. Laughs:
this is all for me.

The hottest days ranked with necessity:
water, eating gummed balls of sweat and mulch
beading the under-curve of her breast,
and on harder flesh,
where the back attaches to wing.
Cicada grew, ate, walked the field,
birthed. She prepares to die,
her wings violins in mantra.

2

I wake up to an enormous announcement
of monsoon's ending,
like rediscovering a wish
I made when I was a girl
that comes true as long as I believe.

Their sound like hundreds of tin cans
twirling on long, thin sticks,

a metal rhythm, hollow and reverberating,
widening, pressing its psychic stain
on every other pulse.

Like this, I know them
from their body-shells left behind,
husks colored in oil slicks
I collect after the last monsoons.

The discreet changeover to autumn.
Perfect casts of their bodies,
at the height of life.

Day of the Dead

I

I can think about this —
burrowed tracks of cicadas
descending further than I
ever imagined. Inward
to a sleeping,
to a dream that will hold them
at a low heart-murmur until they rise,
assumption into the mouth of night.
Toward infinite movement,
and from inside the cramping uterus
of this dugout, beneath the field of corn
I wait.

2

They are all gone, sometimes,
when I do not hear them.
I didn't escape,
won't ever see the world as it was
before the coming,
before this space of earthen walls.

3

My sight is leaving,
the picture of my son's face
dissolves at the narrow crease
of my eyes. I must force
the muscles in my eyelids,
helped by those of the brow,

to fix, hold long enough,
flex, and be still
so that my eyes remember
the way it looked before darkness
marched on me.

4

I sit here beneath the past,
planted like a fresh bone in a trap
to catch foragers of the milpa.
Deep in earth, my scent now blends.
I'm indistinguishable among dank moss,
lichen, mulched weeds, bark
so wet it's soft.
The undersides of all things move, slowly.
This is the part of the day
when it's usual to give in.
Not able to move or make sound.

5

I'll be glad to re-enter the world,
the certainty of where it leads.
It does lead. Away.

6

Coming back from Casa Grande,
a coyote run down, destroyed,
curled on the path.

Then another,
far into the desert field,
chewing through the furred hide

of what keeps her entering and re-entering
the world.

A sign? One successful, one not.

7

I sit rearranging my bones.
Should I raise my head
above the curve of earth
to see if I can leave?

I have no work,
no reason to propel me
further into a long canal,
like my daughter's difficult birth
over the bone ridge,
in an awkward position — her face up,
and a hostile hand turns her
downward for a final descent.

8

When the Spaniards were inside,
laughing and playing floor games
with our clay house gods,
I sat at my husband's butcher table.
The last light of day hung
above the teeth of the western mountain.
My daughter, four days old,
sucked for food,
she and I fragile as webs.

I see the Spaniards,
strange, like their words

I don't recognize,
words that fall . . . no —
words fell. Fell on us.

I don't forget my children's first noises,
how each one tongued the nipple,
the short or long and naked toes
seeking warmth from my silver-ribboned belly.

9

Nobody here has eyes —
only the night's bald eye,
glaring *you!you!you!*
from her blue wall of night.

Soon I'll be where cicadas always sing,
vibrating in their sunken cones.
Their wings brushing against papery armatures,
molds of themselves.

10

Father and mother!
and to the final moon,
the dark face
not able to see me,
where my form finds kinship
with the floating, brittle stars.

My memory is
my children's breath,
torn calluses between my husband's forefinger and thumb,
stones we gathered for a garden of yuccas and magueys
below a crease of sky.

OASIS

My Mother Returns to Calaboz

The Lower Rio Grande, known as the Seno Mexicano (the Mexican Hollow or Recess), was a refuge for rebellious Indians from the Spanish *presidios*, who preferred outlawry to life under Spanish rule.

AMERICO PAREDES, *With His Pistol in His Hand*

The fragmented jawbones
and comblike teeth of seagulls
sometimes wash up from the gulf
to the levee of the river
and gather striated along the berms
where my grandfather irrigated sugarcane.

My mother, returned after forty years away,
walks there often,
hassled by INS agents
when she jogs by the river.
They think she runs away from them,
that she is an illegal,
trespassing from Mexico.
Used to the invasion,
she asks them how they assume,
how *exactly* do they know
if she came from here, or there?
I am an indigenous woman,
born in El Calaboz, you understand?
she says loudly in Spanish,
and they tear out,
the truck wheels spinning furiously,
sand sprayed into the humid air.

When I was a girl walking on the levee,
I thought I saw gull teeth
chomping at the soil wall.
The air was dank steam,
the scent of sand, roots,
and something alive beneath the soil,
deeper and older than memory.
When I immersed my hand inside
the cloudy water,
it became a fluid form,
soft, something becoming,
something ancient.

The air is still heavy with heat and damp,
but smells like diesel and herbicides.
The scent reminds me of failed gestations.
My reproduction, the plants', and the water's,
each struggling in the same web of survival.

When I was a girl, my grandfather taught me
to put a small clump of soil in my mouth,
and to swallow it. I watched him.
Then I did.
I used to watch the gliding and swerves
of uprooted reeds in the river's unhurried flow
to the Gulf.
I reached with all my body,
stomach on the bank of the levee,
hands and arms stretched out like an acrobat
to touch and grasp their slender stems.
Once, my feet pressed into the soupy bog,

and stepping up was the sound of gurgles,
like seaweed breathing.

Now, I think I'd like to be running with my mother
when she tells off *la migra.**
Listen to the bubbling duet of water and plant life,
listen to their sound,
closely.
Again and again.

---

*U.S. Border Patrol. *Migratorio* and *migratoria*
are adjectives that mean "migratory." Perhaps
migra is a derivative of one of these words.

Valentine's Day

Here, the dark sky
and the city between us.
A few classes of English
will hold us over again.
You on the farm every day.
The cries of our babies
behind your head. You recite the list,
make sure I get it over their cranky voices.
Your calmness a rope I will hold
through all the errands —
heater pump for the truck, frozen juice,
diaper pins, Darjeeling. Until I am in the dark
of our bed, your thighs folding mine
under warm blankets,
your nose finding its place
in the crease behind my ear;
Milpa nuzzling for the nipple,
tiny fingers on her free hand strum
the lobe of skin over my ribs.

Again the memory
that you brought chiles for me to preserve.
A coffee can in your rough hands,
you brought your body. In no good condition.
Made me feel that I should learn
to be useful.
You came afflicted,
a thrashed, old suit.
I gave you the key to the front door,
not saying anything.
I handed you other entries, ones without keys,

fists of flowers. You breathe,
dive, open everything in me,
push to the surface, go in again.
Daily the wounds are closing. Smooth pink blossoms.
You find the parts, fix yourself,
the feared dream.
I see how you put things together.
Compare. Say nothing.
Begin the quiet. It is new.
I am new at this attempt at grace.

Smooth Pink Blossoms

We can't repossess the damage we inflict
like replacing one cheap necklace for another.
We are scared of truth, though truth is the only door.

I open, not saying anything
more. Deciding for quiet, for an alternative. Giving you
entrances, the sacred threshold.
My body trumpets the horrific beauty
firmly planted in soil we restore.
I'm curling far over in hard winds.

The body, absent of fairies, a smashed cathedral forest.
Inside my womb, flesh is like July storm skies.

Daily the wounds are closing.
I see you dance within yourself.

I, too, dance alone, invoked. From my perch
our views separate, rejoin;
repossessing myself, I join
life on the exposed forest floor.

The Sound of Doves

I felt your body approach and pause
between the door and the hallway. I am in the bath,
the length of my body folded to fit,
and parts of me submerged. I watch a delicate form.
Thin layers of bubbles attach themselves
to the fine hairs of my body.

My hand glides an arc, a deep, fine furrow
around my stomach, a tree of veins.

I see as if outside the body.
Beneath frayed cuticles, unshaven legs,
this crescent mound. The tiny streams breaking, layering.
Skin like rough terrain, and
water not enough to cover all the stretches
from pregnancies and births.

You ask me to show myself.
Layering folds of skin from the births
of our children, this scar above my brow
that points to the sky,
fine hairs from the navel forming a passage
to dark magentas in the center of my womb.

I hear doves through the crumbling ceiling,
flutter their wings
like sprays of water.

I hear their muffled cries in my shivering body,
letting forth
like an uncertain chorus.

I listen to your breath
moving over my skin
like tiny wings.

Oasis

The once beneficial rain had been changed,
through the evil power of the poison introduced
into their world, into an agent of destruction.

    RACHEL CARSON, *Silent Spring*

> *I am a thin string,*
> I say to my friend,
> *it is a good sign, normality, sanity,*
> *to be depressed.* If a person
> does *not* admit the peril:
> scarcity of safe water,
> the family sprayed with chemicals
> each cotton season,
> our mutations, and our dead;
> species, children, mothers
> decimated everywhere,
> *that* becomes a dangerous
> form of existence. Mirage.
>
> I have to weigh the wreckage.
> The large farms around us heavy in herbicides.
> Friends and friends of friends.
>
> We buried our miscarried child.
> My stomach a bag,
> sagging its dread
> for want of something to carry.
>
> I went around our small farm,
> frantic for my three-year-old's blanket.
> A year I embroidered
> our Eden on the flannel.

Any effort towards anything good
was in the French knots,
the ice-green of arrow-weed,
puffed globe mallows
leaning their orange, silk mouths
on yuccas in chain and slip stitch;
a young hawk we saw above the field,

descending with absolute faith.
His plummeting eye
I rendered in loops and tassels
from memory —
my authority.

The blanket pushing into my brain stem,
points blame to everyone.
Where is it? What do you remember?

A long time, after much cursing,
the blanket, covered by dried leaves,
is found behind the adobe hut. When does
one thing begin and another end?

I recall my stiff fingers
moving across the gauze-cotton weave,
at night, or when my husband
was gone on faraway travel.
My hands crawled as if out of a coma,
struggled to remember themselves.
In a vigil, I hunched

over the embroidery hoop.
My stitchery the story
since our first daughter's birth.

A design of artifacts, absences:
my dead father,
my living mother,
children I've buried
and those alive,
my husband, far off, in the garden.

Then, the absences I desire.
Secret little invertebrates I see in the mirror,
grotesque and screwing each other,
growling a howl of the neglected.

The honey locust outside,
all its hundred rippled pods
like cracked lips
and the color of dried blood.
Trembling leaves of the harvest fade,
rattling *this all returns*.

God is a snowbird.
"Each time I think it is here
that God lives."*
In my mean mind I forget.

My children laugh outside,
strip off their clothes,

piss under the fig tree,
dance to reggae.

They keep their centrality.

I wonder
if I ever had security.

I gaze at the dark and cool sky.
When I prayed for rain,
a monsoon came.

Thunderbolts drummed a warning of imminent floods,
the children ran to the slide,
their mud-covered bodies hydroplaning on
the slippery band of metal and
across long, wide puddles growing larger,
their faces and hands open and reaching,
five of them linked hands to ankles,
skidding and scraping knees and elbows
in the shallow, sandy mud.

ı TERRAIN

I am watching the sky,
a disciple,
on my knees,
raw from the fall.
Colder than I can remember,
believing the faithful
will find their refuge.

I am holding out
for resolution. Holding out
for a decent effort, returning to my life
like these Gambel's sparrows who return
to fallen seeds each morning.

Last week my father died.
I taught Olds' "35/10"
to freshmen.

For my parents at home,
their 25th year together,
I spoke the poem on video.

I believed
I was figuring things out,
though the tape, wrapped, addressed,
sat with the bills and subscriptions

I forgot to pay.
My father never saw it.

I spoke at his funeral,
my mind on ovaries, ova,
delayed decisions.
I envied that he was spirit,
lifting off.

My students watch me
the first morning back.
Their eyes to the poems,
then back to my face.
I sense their need for cues.
I'll read where we left off.

I am hoarse. My voice dribbles,
crawls up to their feet,
fluorescent bulbs amplify
the four feet between us.
I'm sorry, let me begin again.

Start with men and women,
persecuted and dying.
Europe's torture camps.
Unnamed landscapes of soil, trees,
mutilations, massacres, desecration.

Eyes of motherhood,
soft folds of skin
on a small child's decomposing body,
delicate and thin strands of veins

on an old man's brow.
He strains and gasps
against his executors.

To their stunned faces I want to say,
stagger into me.
The gorge.
A scorch in my bowels.
Admit the damage.
The bodies meticulously documented.
Memorize this.

I LANDMARKS

I go home. Shelter: his kiss,
cornfield, hot bath, corn bread, beans,
squash pie, tamales, canned tomatoes,
children, hot tea,
stories, nurse a baby,
clean the kids, burn a candle,
sleep.

My father comes to me,
the first dream
in four months of dream.
He talks to me from his ornate Cadillac-blue casket.
This is casual. I'm amazed
at how well I take it,
repelled by the way I take it.
He knows. It's ok.
I wake and know
I've been somewhere.
There is sweat on my brow,
my breasts, my neck.
My husband stirs,
reaches for me in darkness.

but it's 5:00 A.M., time to go.
Preparation. The body
set to function,
get up, get dressed,
leave.

I drive. The bleak
dark of pre-dawn is cryptic.
Thinking of the dream,
I am stupefied by my father's question:
Why am I still here?

His attempt to reach back,
losing time, the constellations tick
across the vault.

Distant lights of Phoenix
like a delicate strand of gold beads
against the dark throat of the city.
Dawn's ruby-violet lips
spread and swallow
the gel of night.

ı MAPPING

Turning off the highway I think:
when does everyone wake up?

Over public radio,
refugee children in Rwanda.
Separated —
a diaspora into Zaire,
unable to reunite
with their parents or families.
Small children say
in raspy, swollen voices that
they struggle to survive brutalities
—being lost on Earth.
Their strength a faint hope that
reconnection can one day
be possible.
One by one they give testimony
to genocide.

One voice. A child.
His sounds like rusty keys
thudding against one another on a loop.
Says he remembers his father's name
but can't remember,
after two years of being lost,
the name of his village.
Another quiet voice speaks
a melodic language,
the sound in his mouth, from his lips
a gathering of leaves and reed wind,
something nearing an end,
or emergence.

ᛁ EAT, DRINK

I see the sun stretch its long, amber back
against the desert, mountains,
remember dying old men
decrepit, exquisite,
children's voices shrill, starved.

I go to the city
to teach in a building.
This is a building of concrete
to perpetuate, to preserve, to contain, to buttress, to empower.
I can hear the buzz of machines
when I walk the corridor to my office.

I sit at my desk.
Try to be warm, though I still shiver.

In this room are desks like mine.
Castoffs of tenured faculty and former teachers,
pictures of children or spouses, lovers or heroes,
parents with love, posters with bold phrases,
venerated anarchists, Buddha shrines,
Che Guevara, stacks of books, memos, reminders,
essays in boxes collecting dust.

Who wants to say something . . . ?
At the end of the hall
my palms hit the door handles flat,
cold metal sends a stinging erosion
through my fingers that radiates outward
like fronds of a date palm

into the twilight. Frigid air shoves
its wild severity into my lungs.

The Gambel's sparrows compete
for pomegranate seed, blister-red,
on the manicured lawn.
Their head stripes, small black and white blades,
shave the air.
Raw from the fall,
watching the red-streaked sky, a disciple,
I rise and wipe rough
eucalyptus pods from my scraped knees,
knowing the test is not over.

The Collection

for Maura Luna Squash Blossom

Chili pods wintered over,
shriveled like old toes in a bath —
their stems brittle as amber
that would snap apart at the touch.
They will save in Tarahumara baskets
for seed and grinding.

Aztec blue corn, dried on the stalk.
We let the weeds get away.
Rodents and crows had their share.
I rub each cob in a wringing motion,
old calluses wake up.
Kernels fall into the pan,
pinging like hard rain
on the metal roof.

Saving these seeds, I feel a peace
that many lives got what they needed
and gave back.
A micro-landscape was fed and enlarged.
When these night-blue kernels
rub my fingers raw,
when I am tired of doing this
and it hurts,
I'm mad
that I want to quit.

People's faces appear. I go on.
This corn came heirloomed,

grandmothered and grandfathered,
to me, us.
The corn breathed air, drank water,
smaller lives ate the compost,
their shit and heat and life made the humus
that fed it.
I will eat.

The soreness will go away.
My hands twist and rasp
one cob against another.
I reach for two more
from the basket piled high
with a day's full work.

Your hair as you sleep is crow-feather night,
strands of thread
under the small swell of my breast;

the mockingbird on the telephone pole,
his throat snatching breeze,
swallows a sliver of chemical-air;

clouds, heavy and dark as skillets,
the steam of their good work rising;

in the stomach of a cottonwood,
wings of a hundred cicadas
shiver as one;

crows skim a low shadow across a wet furrow,
arch their slick bodies
at the skeletal dome of the sweat lodge;

a beetle pauses
at the edge of a dog's divot in the sand,
tamps, keeps pausing,
waits for a decision;

my daughter,
her language beginning with *buh,*
chants and escalates her cries,
food! love! more!

the mango's slow trickle
off my lip-crease
unravels itself down to my elbow;

all like:
chickens vibrating their frog-throats,
my son, beneath dark clouds, dances their beats,
the rasp of his throaty prize.

Between These Worlds

I've seen them clear fences at night
in front of cars doing fifty
on a two-lane road.

They gallop across and leap through headlight funnels,
into a thin fog between this world
and a sloping berm of dark.

My husband says the herds
are led by the wild
spirit horses with light eyes.

I believe this.
We used to hear
their racing hooves
near our window
on waxing-moon nights.

We thought that was their way
of accepting us
in the desert valley.

We were in bed,
being still to listen,
to feel the vibrations
of their hooves breaking
the soil.

I stood up on the bed
to look out the window,
moonlight showing stiff stands of foxtail.

I return. My husband pulls up the blanket,
his long leg over my hip,
fastening me to him and this world.
Though he drifted off,
I couldn't, still wondering.

Now, I don't hear them
at night
moonlit or not.
There is less magic
without a galloping announcement
of resistance.

Dark clouds pass
silently over the mountain.
The huge stone moves
toward the herd. Highlanders
all winter. Yuccas and cholla
nudge them inward to shallow arroyos
where they feed.

I see them from the kitchen window,
though they are far.
Muzzles nibbling the wild rye
where the fog drapes the mountain.

On the Wing

The blue martins snatch
damselflies and stinkbugs
as they drift an evening thermal.
The largest of swallows, their size
all in the tail.

I'm hanging laundry in autumn
late in the day,
stiff shadows of clothespins,
their oblique angle to earth,
and their large V-forms
oddly like martins
dipping and braiding for food.
With the blue martins' return,
I surrender all my fear
to a past I can't dismiss.
I won't speak, nor forecast,
nor ask for a thing,
but just watch them
as they pull lavender-plum threads of evening
through the fiery kiln of sundown.

Tonight I'm praying for the buffalo
trailing that aurora,
a sky where night is day
and day is night and

what we say is dust
and what we can never say
goes into a prayer,
where I am you

and you are me
and we move this
into a spirit of the herd.

And when the herd returns
we'll be hanging laundry on the line,
we'll be watching sparrows and doves,
we'll be listening to the children,
when the herd returns
we'll be painting the ancestors,
we'll be teaching under ironwoods in blossom,
we'll be suckling on our mothers' soft breasts,
when the herd returns
we'll be asking for peace,
we'll be asking for a blessing,
we'll be making peace with our mothers,
when the herd returns
we'll make bread for our fathers and learn to plant corn,
we'll share our bounty with those who didn't plant,
we'll eliminate poverty and hunger,
when the herd returns
we'll live with less,
we'll birth babies at home,
we'll sing them welcome songs when they crown,
when the herd returns
we'll be singing to bring rain,
singing to heal our grief,
singing to the moon.

I make a prayer for us.
That we'll be singing like Inca doves,
that we'll be watching swallows on a thermal flow,
that we'll *be* the swallows eating dragonflies on the wing
when the herd returns.

Hummingbirds Compete for the Tobacco Tree

How can I understand that what is absent is not gone,
that what has ended is not finished,
that what is taken is returned
as more than memory?

SUSAN HANSON, *"Why Write about Nature?"*

Their flute-bodies wind the trunk
of a tobacco tree shading me
as I clean some seed from the chaff.

The tobacco's yellow flowers,
tassels gathered at each stem,
heave and swell
on waves of heat.
I show my children how
to clean the nectar from the delicate tube,
ripe for sucking.

The hummers,
like tiny missiles under my arm.
I reach to them,
arms and hands to hold,
carry. Gather me to loved ones.

The hummers skim the wide wood footholds
near the mud-splattered spigot.
I laugh at their chase,
surprised by their precision,
how they attack without thought
for their own hunger.

Under this tree
the shade is a loose lace
of blank eyes
quaking on July's baked ground.

The hundred yellow bugle-blooms
shrug off summer.

Outside the fringe of shade,
Earth shifts a scorched shoulder,
plunges, eyes away from the hot god.

Cool above in the vault,
thin strands of lately gone souls
stretch out above us. My father,
who lately made his journey,
is out there too.

I wave to him.
He wears vintage clothes.
Leans against a spotless
teal '57 sedan, smiling.

He tells the dearly not-departed
to keep cooking eggs and potatoes,
make tortillas in a good mood.
Bathe the kids and comb the knots from their hair . . .
Look at my eyes in the mirror longer.

Forgive. Make love.

Go to the desert and howl
the body's compressed grief.

Gather ironwood kindling
to make a fire. Look under decaying
cholla or mesquites for mulch
to catch the flame.

Blow steady breaths on the fragile glow.
Feed it, stay there.
Look at the eyes in the fire.

Before it's over,
when maybe everything almost is,
offer little branches
to crumbling coals
of naked wanting.

Margo Tamez received her M.F.A. in Poetry at the Creative Writing Program at Arizona State University. She is the recipient of regional and national awards, including a Poetry Fellowship from the Arizona Commission on the Arts in 1999, the poetry award from the *Frontera Literary Review*, an award from the Environmental Leadership Program, and a Distinguished Achievement award from the Alice Longon Foundation. Her work has appeared in *American Poetry Review, Cimarron Review, Hawaii Pacific Review, The Peace Review, Americas Review,* and other journals, as well as anthologies. Margo Tamez lives and works in Maricopa, Arizona, at De Las Manos Center for Peace and Environment Studies with her husband and children.